A Commentary on the United Nations
Convention on the Rights of the Child

Editors

André Alen, Johan Vande Lanotte, Eugeen Verhellen,
Fiona Ang, Eva Berghmans and Mieke Verheyde

Article 31

The Right to Leisure, Play and Culture

By

Paulo David

Regional Representative, Office of the United Nations
High Commissioner for Human Rights (OHCHR)
and former Secretary of the UN Committee on the Rights of the
Child (1995–2005)

MARTINUS NIJHOFF PUBLISHERS
LEIDEN • BOSTON
2006

This book is printed on acid-free paper.

A Cataloging-in-Publication record for this book is available from the Library of Congress.

Cite as: P. David "Article 31: The Right to Leisure, Play and Culture", in: A. Alen, J. Vande Lanotte, E. Verhellen, F. Ang, E. Berghmans and M. Verheyde (Eds.) *A Commentary on the United Nations Convention on the Rights of the Child* (Martinus Nijhoff Publishers, Leiden, 2006).

ISSN 1574-8626
ISBN 13: 978-90-04-14882-6
ISBN 10: 90-04-14882-5

© 2006 by Koninklijke Brill NV, Leiden, The Netherlands.
Koninklijke Brill NV incorporates the imprints Brill Academic Publishers, Martinus Nijhoff Publishers and VSP.

Cover image by Nadia, 1 $^1/_2$ years old

http://www.brill.nl

PRINTED IN THE NETHERLANDS

CONTENTS

LIST OF ABBREVIATIONS

CRC	UN Convention on the Rights of the Child, 1989
ICCPR	UN International Covenant on Civil and Political Rights, 1966
ICESCR	UN International Covenant on Economic, Social and Cultural Rights, 1966
ILO	International Labour Organisation
IPA	International Association for the Child's Right to Play
UDHR	Universal Declaration of Human Rights, 1948
UNESCO	UN Educational, Scientific and Cultural Organisation
UNICEF	UN Children's Fund

AUTHOR BIOGRAPHY

Paulo David was born in 1962 in the Netherlands and holds both Dutch and Swiss nationalities. He is currently Regional Representative, Office of the United Nations High Commissioner for Human Rights (OHCHR). From 1995 to 2005 he was Secretary of the UN Committee on the Rights of the Child (1995–2005). Mr. David started his career in 1985 as a journalist before working for the International Federation of Red Cross and Red Crescent Societies in Romania and Turkey (1990–1991). Thereafter he joined Defence for Children International (DCI) before moving to the United Nations. Paulo David holds a PhD in Law from the Free University of Amsterdam and is the author of numerous publications. 'Human Rights in Youth Sport. A critical review of children's rights in competitive sport' (London, Routledge, 2005) is his most recent book.

TEXT OF ARTICLE 31

ARTICLE 31

1. States Parties recognize the right of the child to rest and leisure, to engage in play and recreational activities appropriate to the age of the child and to participate freely in cultural life and the arts.

2. States Parties shall respect and promote the right of the child to participate fully in cultural and artistic life and shall encourage the provision of appropriate and equal opportunities for cultural, artistic, recreational and leisure activity.

ARTICLE 31

1. Les Etats parties reconnaissent à l'enfant le droit au repos et aux loisirs, de se livrer au jeu et à des activités récréatives propres à son âge et de participer librement à la vie culturelle et artistique.

2. Les Etats parties respectent et favorisent le droit de l'enfant de participer pleinement à la vie culturelle et artistique et encouragent l'organisation à son intention de moyens appropriés de loisirs et d'activités récréatives, artistiques et culturelles, dans des conditions d'égalité.

CHAPTER ONE

INTRODUCTION*

1. The right to rest and leisure, to engage in play and recreational activity and to participate fully in cultural and artistic life is recognized in Article 31 of the Convention on the Rights of the Child (CRC). With the exception of the right to play, other specific rights recognized in this provision have been previously recognized to all – adults and children alike – in other international instruments, including the 1966 International Covenant on Economic, Social and Cultural Rights (CESCR).

2. Interpretation of Article 31 is mainly inspired by the *Travaux Préparatoires* of the CRC, jurisprudence of international human rights treaty bodies, academic and other literature on international human rights and other instruments and on treaty bodies work, research on children's rights, policy declarations of various organisations and, when existing, domestic jurisprudence.

* September 2005.

CHAPTER TWO

COMPARISON WITH RELATED INTERNATIONAL HUMAN RIGHTS PROVISIONS

3. Article 31 of the CRC encompasses different but closely related specific rights recognized to children: a) the right to rest; b) the right to leisure; c) the right to play and recreation; and d) the right to participate freely in cultural life and the arts.

4. These four components of Article 31 are not reflected in a consistent and homogenous way in international and regional instruments. If a large variety of instruments refer explicitly to the right to rest and leisure: they overwhelmingly do it in the particular and restricted context of working conditions. Only child rights instruments do articulate these rights in a broader sense. Further, some regional instruments, such as the European Social Charter and the Arab Charter on Human Rights do recognize the right to rest, but not the right to leisure.

5. Particular attention should be paid to the fact that the right to play is a new type of right which was for the first time recognized in the CRC and thereafter in the African Charter. It is therefore a right only acknowledged under international law for persons below 18. No other human rights instruments do recognize this right, though some soft law instruments do promote the right to play (Cf. infra. para. 62).

1. Right to Rest and Leisure

6. Article 31 is greatly inspired by the CESCR which recognizes rights in these domains for children and adults alike. Its Article 7(d) states:

> 'The States Parties to the present Covenant recognize the right of everyone to the enjoyment of just and favourable conditions of work which ensure, in particular: [. . .]
>
> (d) Rest, leisure and reasonable limitation of working hours and periodic holidays with pay, as well as remuneration for public holidays.'

7. The Covenant recognizes the right to rest and leisure in the context of work exclusively, contrary to the CRC which does not explicitly link Article 31 to a specific situation or setting, rather leaving the matter open. As seen later (*Cf. infra* No. 37), Article 31 of the CRC can be closely associated to many other provisions of the treaty, including the right to development of children (Article 6(2)), the right to education (Articles 28 and 29) and the right to be protected from economic exploitation and benefit of appropriate conditions of employment (Article 32).

8. The Covenant itself was inspired by the 'mother human rights treaty', the 1948 Universal Declaration of Human Rights (which is not of legally binding nature). Its Article 24 recognizes that:

> 'Everyone has the right to rest and leisure, including reasonable limitation of working hours and periodic holidays with pay.'

Again, this right is directly associated to working conditions.

9. The Convention on the Elimination of All Forms of Discrimination against Women (CEDAW) prohibits any form of discrimination against girls and women, including in the fields of economic, social and cultural rights. Its Article 13 affirms:

> 'States Parties shall take all appropriate measures to eliminate discrimination against women in other areas of economic and social life in order to ensure, on a basis of equality of men and women, the same rights, in particular: [...]
>
> (c) The right to participate in recreational activities, sports and all aspects of cultural life.'

10. Two International Labour Organization (ILO) conventions specifically protect children from working at night and stipulate the number of hours of consecutive rest children should have: children under 14 or in full-time education should have 14 hours' rest per day; those aged 14 to 16, 12 hours; and adolescents aged 16 to 18, at least seven hours (ILO Conventions Nos. 79 and 90). ILO 1946 Convention No. 79 concerning the Restriction of Night Work of Children and Young Persons in Non-Industrial Occupations states (Article 2):

> 1. Children under fourteen years of age who are admissible for full-time or part-time employment and children over fourteen years of age who are still subject to full-time compulsory school attendance shall not be employed nor work at night during a period of at least fourteen consecutive hours,

including the interval between eight o'clock in the evening and eight o'clock in the morning.'

11. ILO 1948 Convention No. 90 concerning the Night Work of Young Persons Employed in Industry states (Article 2):

> 3. In the case of young persons who have attained the age of sixteen years but are under the age of eighteen years, this period shall include an interval prescribed by the competent authority of at least seven consecutive hours falling between ten o'clock in the evening and seven o'clock in the morning; the competent authority may prescribe different intervals for different areas, industries, undertakings or branches of industries or undertakings, but shall consult the employers' and workers' organisations concerned before prescribing an interval beginning after eleven o'clock in the evening.'

12. The 1988 Additional Protocol to the American Convention on Human Rights in the area of Economic, Social and Cultural Rights (Protocol of San Salvador) also links the right to rest and leisure to work. Its Article 7 states:

> 'The States Parties to this Protocol recognize that the right to work to which the foregoing article refers presupposes that everyone shall enjoy that right under just, equitable, and satisfactory conditions, which the States Parties undertake to guarantee in their internal legislation, particularly with respect to: [. . .]

> h. Rest, leisure and paid vacations as well as remuneration for national holidays.'

13. In its Article 12, the 1990 African Charter on the Rights and Welfare of the Child uses exactly the same wording as Article 31 of the CRC.

14. The European Social Charter refers to the right to rest in its Article 2 entitled 'the right to just conditions of work', but not to the right to leisure. Article 2 reads as follows:

> 'With a view to ensuring the effective exercise of the right to just conditions of work, the Contracting Parties undertake: [. . .]

> (5) to ensure a weekly rest period which shall, as far as possible, coincide with the day recognised by tradition or custom in the country or region concerned as a day of rest.'

15. The Arab Charter on Human Rights[1] recognizes the right to rest in the context of work. Its Article 34, para. 2 states:

---

[1] The revised Charter was adopted by the Arab League during 2004 and has not yet entered into force (1 September 2005).

'Every worker has the right to the enjoyment of just and favourable
conditions of work which ensure appropriate remuneration to meet his
essential needs and those of his family and regulate working hours, rest
and holidays with pay.'

2. Right to Play and Recreation

16. Unlike the right to rest and leisure and the right to participate freely
in cultural life, the right to play and recreation is only recognized with
regard to children. In addition to the CRC, the African Charter is the only
other international or regional treaty recognizing this right and the
wording of Article 12 of the Charter reproduces exactly the text of
the CRC.

3. Right to Participate Freely in Cultural Life and the Arts

17. The right to participate freely in cultural life and the arts is also
anchored in the Universal Declaration of Human Rights (UDHR) and the
1966 International Covenant on Economic, Social and Cultural Rights.
Article 27 of the UDHR states that:

> '1. Everyone has the right freely to participate in the cultural life of the
>   community, to enjoy the arts and to share in scientific advancement
>   and its benefits.
>
> 2. Everyone has the right to the protection of the moral and material
>   interests resulting from any scientific, literary or artistic production of
>   which he is the author.'

18. Article 15 of the CESCR is also relevant as it says:

> '1. The States Parties to the present Covenant recognize the right of everyone:
>   (a) To take part in cultural life;
>   (b) To enjoy the bits of scientific progress and its applications;
>   (c) To benefit from the protection of the moral and material interests
>   resulting from any scientific, literary or artistic production of which
>   he is the author.
>
> 2. The steps to be taken by the States Parties to the present Covenant to
>   achieve the full realization of this right shall include those necessary
>   for the conservation, the development and the diffusion of science and
>   culture.
>
> 3. The States Parties to the present Covenant undertake to respect the
>   freedom indispensable for scientific research and creative activity.

4. The States Parties to the present Covenant recognize the benefits to be derived from the encouragement and development of international contacts and co-operation in the scientific and cultural fields.'

19. The UDHR specifies that the right to freely participate in cultural life is related to 'the community' whilst the CRC does not provide such specification. Both the UDHR and the CESCR further explicitly recognize the right to share in scientific advancement (or progress) and its benefits (or applications), which is not recognized in the CRC. Both treaties also recognize the right to protection of intellectual property rights of authors which also does not appear in the CRC.

The International Convention on the Elimination of All Forms of Discrimination (CERD) recognizes the right to be protected from all forms of racial discrimination in the enjoyment of 'economic social and cultural rights' (Article 5(e)), including 'the right to equal participation in cultural activities' (Article 5(e)(vi)). In addition, CEDAW prohibits discrimination against women in economic and social life, in order to ensure equality in the enjoyment of the right to participate in all aspects of cultural life (Article 13(c)) (*Cf. supra* No. 9).

Article 14 of the American Convention on Human Rights in the area of Economic, Social and Cultural Rights (Protocol of San Salvador) is entirely based on the relevant provisions of the UDHR and the CESCR:

'1. The States Parties to this Protocol recognize the right of everyone:
   a. To take part in the cultural and artistic life of the community;
   b. To enjoy the benefits of scientific and technological progress;
   c. To benefit from the protection of moral and material interests deriving from any scientific, literary or artistic production of which he is the author.

2. The steps to be taken by the States Parties to this Protocol to ensure the full exercise of this right shall include those necessary for the conservation, development and dissemination of science, culture and art.

3. The States Parties to this Protocol undertake to respect the freedom indispensable for scientific research and creative activity.

4. The States Parties to this Protocol recognize the benefits to be derived from the encouragement and development of international cooperation and relations in the fields of science, arts and culture, and accordingly agree to foster greater international cooperation in these fields.'

20. As seen under 'Right to rest and leisure' (*Cf. supra* No. 16), Article 12 of the African Charter on the Rights and Welfare of the Child exactly mirrors Article 31 of the CRC.

21. In its Article 42(3), the Arab Charter on Human Rights commits States Parties to:

> '[...] work together and enhance cooperation among them at all levels, with the full participation of intellectuals and inventors and their organizations, in order to develop and implement recreational, cultural, artistic and scientific programmes.'

22. Finally, it should be noted that in 1976, the United Nations Educational, Scientific and Cultural Organisation (UNESCO) adopted a non-binding instrument entitled 'Recommendation on Participation by the People at Large in Cultural Life and their Contribution to It' that provides elements of definition of the 'right to participate freely in cultural life and the arts.'

CHAPTER THREE

SCOPE OF ARTICLE 31

1. *Brief Historical Perspective*

23. The original proposal of the CRC submitted by Poland to the UN Commission on Human Rights in 1978 (34th session) did not include any reference to the right to rest and leisure or to participate freely in cultural life and the arts.

24. The text only referred to 'play and recreation'. Article VII of the original proposal of the Convention read as follows:[2]

> 'The child is entitled to receive education, which shall be free and compulsory, at least in the elementary stages. He shall be given an education which will promote his general culture and enable him, on a basis of equal opportunity, to develop his abilities, his individual judgement, and his sense of moral and social responsibility, and to become a useful member of society.
>
> The best interests of the child shall be the guiding principle of those responsible for his education and guidance; that responsibility lies in the first place with his parents.
>
> The child shall have full opportunity for play and recreation, which should be directed to the same purposes as education; society and the public authorities shall endeavour to promote the enjoyment of this right.'

25. The Government of Canada proposed in 1983 to include in the original text a reference to the 'right to rest and leisure, to engage in play and recreation and to freely participate in cultural life.'[3] This proposal was discussed during the eighties by the Working Group established by the UN Commission on Human Rights to negotiate the text of the CRC and progressively evolved towards the final text of Article 31, adopted in 1989.[4]

---

[2] *Travaux Préparatoires* (UN Doc. E/CN.4/L.1366, 1978).
[3] *Travaux Préparatoires* (UN Doc. E/CN/4/1983/62, Annex II (E/CN.4/1983/WG.1/WP.26) and UN Doc. E/CN.4/1984/71, Annex II, p. 2).
[4] S. Detrick (ed.) *The United Nations Convention on the Rights of the Child. A Guide to the Travaux Préparatoires* (Dordrecht/Boston/London, Martinus Nijhoff Publishers, 1992), pp. 414–418.

Detrick affirms that the 'CRC's *travaux préparatoires* show the intended aim of the particular rights of the child laid down in Article 31 is to promote and protect the child's development within the context of the child's community as well as the child's school and family'.[5]

2. *Nature of State Obligations*

26. The nature of State Parties' obligations under Article 31 is formulated in the use of the term 'recognize' in paragraph 1 of the provision. In paragraph 2, the terms 'respect and promote' are also used, though not in relation to the rights to play and rest, as these surprisingly do not appear in paragraph 2. An explanation might be that the drafters of the treaty considered that the right to rest is included in the right to leisure and the right to play is covered by the right to recreational activities. The term 'recognize' is used in several other provisions of the CRC and in most of the CESCR, including in its related Articles 7(d) and Article 15(1)(a). Under the CRC, 'recognition' of a right and related uses of the terms 'respect and promote' relate directly to Article 4 of the CRC that states:

> 'States Parties shall undertake all appropriate legislative, administrative, and other measures for the implementation of the rights recognized in the present Convention. With regard to economic, social and cultural rights, States Parties shall undertake such measures to the maximum extent of their available resources and, where needed, within the framework of international co-operation.'[6]

27. In its General Comment No. 5 on the 'General measures of Implementation of the Convention on the Rights of the Child (Articles 4, 42 and 44 (6))',[7] the CRC Committee[8] provides further explanations on the

---

[5] S. Detrick, *A Commentary on the United Nations Convention on the Rights of the Child* (The Hague, Kluwer Academic Publishers Group, 1999), p. 547.

[6] For an in-depth analysis of the content and meaning of Article 4 of the CRC, see M. Rishmawi, 'Article 4. The Nature of States Parties' Obligations', in: A. Alen, J. Vande Lanotte, E. Verhellen, F. Ang, E. Berghmans and M. Verheyde (eds.), *A Commentary on the United Nations Convention on the Rights of the Child* (Leiden, Martinus Nijhoff Publishers, 2006).

[7] CRC Committee, *General Comments No. 5: General Measures of Implementation of the Convention on the Rights of the Child* (UN Doc. CRC/GC/2003/5, 2003).

[8] The Committee on the Rights of the Child was established in 1991 under Article 43 of the CRC 'for the purpose of examining the progress made by States Parties in achieving the realization of the obligations undertaken in the [present] Convention.'

measures States Parties need to take in order to fulfil their obligations under the CRC. In particular, the Committee explains what it expects from every State Party under the requirement of Article 4 of the CRC. They are required to 'undertake all appropriate legislative, administrative, and other measures for the implementation of the rights recognized in the present Convention'.

28. The Committee expects States Parties to the CRC to explicitly recognize in domestic legislation the requirements of Article 31, and it might criticize States that have not done so.[9] Notably, the Committee affirms that State obligations have to be implemented within its jurisdiction free of any kind of discrimination.[10] It also stipulates that, despite the specific reference in Article 4 to the fact that 'with regard to economic, social and cultural rights, States Parties shall undertake such measures to the maximum extent of their available resources', the 'enjoyment of economic, social and cultural rights is inextricably intertwined with enjoyment of civil and political rights (. . . .) the Committee believes that economic, social and cultural rights, as well as civil and political rights, should be regarded as justiciable.'[11] This means that lack of resources cannot bluntly justify the non respect of rights recognized in the CRC, including Article 31, as long as the demonstration has not been made that resources to this end have been stretched to their maximum potential. States are in any circumstances required to take measures to implement economic, social and cultural rights.[12] Further, insufficient or improper use of resources by a given State cannot on its own prevent CRC rights from not being justiciable. The Committee on Economic, Social and Cultural Rights adopted an almost similar position as it affirms:[13]

'The fact that realization over time, or in other words progressively, is foreseen under the Covenant should not be misinterpreted as depriving the obligation of all meaningful content. It is on the one hand a necessary

---

[9] See, for example, CRC Committee, *Concluding Observations: Saint Lucia* (UN Doc. CRC/C/15/Add.257, 2005), paras. 64–65.

[10] CRC Committee, *o.c.* (note 7), para. 3.

[11] *Ibid.*, para. 6.

[12] M. Santos Pais, 'The Convention on the rights of the Child', in: Office of the UN High Commissioner for Human Rights, UN Institute for Training and Research and UN Staff College (eds.), *Manual on Human Rights Reporting under Six Major International Human Rights Instruments* (Geneva, Office of the UN High Commissioner for Human Rights, UN Institute for Training and Research and UN Staff College, 1997), p. 409.

[13] CESCR Committee, *General Comment No. 3: The Nature of States Parties Obligations* (UN Doc. E/1991/23, 1991), paras. 9 and 11.

flexibility device, reflecting the realities of the real world and the difficulties involved for any country in ensuring full realization of economic,
social and cultural rights. On the other hand, the phrase must be read in
the light of the overall objective, indeed the *raison d'être*, of the Covenant
which is to establish clear obligations for States parties in respect of the
full realization of the rights in question. It thus imposes an obligation to
move as expeditiously and effectively as possible towards that goal [. . .]
The Committee wishes to emphasize, however, that even where the available resources are demonstrably inadequate, the obligation remains for a
State party to strive to ensure the widest possible enjoyment of the relevant rights under the prevailing circumstances.'

29. Article 2(1) of the CESCR indicates that:

'Each State Party to the present Covenant undertakes to take steps, indi-
vidually and through international assistance and co-operation, especially
economic and technical, to the maximum of its available resources, with
a view to achieving *progressively* the full realisation of the rights recognized
in the present Covenant by all appropriate means, including particularly
the adoption of legislative measures.'[14]

30. This provision means that under this treaty States Parties are obliged
to engage their resources to the maximum extent available to progressively implement the provisions of the CESCR, including the rights to rest,
leisure and participation in cultural life. The CRC does not refer to progressive realisation of rights in an overarching provision similar to Article
2(1) of the CESCR. The CRC refers to progressive realisation only under
the specific right to health (Article 24) and the one to education (Article
28), but not to the other provisions of the treaty. Therefore Article 31,
as well as all other provisions of the treaty with the exception of Articles
24 and 28 of the CRC, requires States Parties to take all measures to
ensure as immediately as possible full realisation of rights recognized in
this provision.[15]

31. In its reporting guidelines for periodic reports, the Committee insists
on obtaining information on 'the proportion of the relevant overall
budget allocated (at the central, regional, local and where relevant at
the federal and provincial levels) for children' for the fields covered by

---

[14] Emphasis added by author.
[15] See also T. Hammarberg, 'Children', in: A. Eide *et al.* (eds), *Economic, Social and Cultural Rights*, 2nd ed. (Dordrecht, Boston, London, Kluwer Law International, 2001), p. 367.

Article 31. Obviously, allocation of appropriate budgetary resources is crucial in order to provide for the 'provision of appropriate and equal opportunities for cultural, artistic, recreational and leisure activity' as spelled out in Article 31(2). Equal access to these activities is a significant concern of the CRC Committee in this context,[16] the same way it is a significant issue tackled by the Committee on Economic, Social and Cultural Rights when addressing the right to participate in cultural life under Article 15 of the CESCR.[17]

32. Importantly, Article 4 of the CRC also requires States Parties 'when needed' to use the various channels of international cooperation to ensure implementation of economic, social and cultural rights. This means that recipient States need to allocate part of the financial and other support received through international cooperation to the implementation of these rights, and not ignore or neglect them in this process. Similarly, donor States also need to ensure that part of their international aid is allocated to this end, from the initiation to the realisation of the process generated by international cooperation.

33. The Committee also considers that when implementing their obligations under the Convention, States Parties need to ensure that the four general principles of the treaty are systematically respected: the right to non-discrimination (Article 2), the principle of the best interests of the child (Article 3), the right to life, survival and development (Article 6) and the right of the child to express his or her views freely 'in all matters affecting the child' (Article 12).[18] In this respect the Committee emphasizes the obligation of States Parties to ensure easy and equal access to the rights enshrined in Article 31, including by taking specific measures for 'children who live in remote and rural areas, disabled children or children belonging to vulnerable groups.'[19]

34. The issue of privatisation of (public) services also relates to the nature of State obligations. In the context of Article 31, public services can be

---

[16] See for example, CRC Committee, *Concluding Observations: Jamaica* (UN Doc. CRC/C/15/Add.210, 2003), para. 48.

[17] S. Yee, 'The "right to take part in cultural life" under article 15 of ICESCR', *International Comparative Law Quarterly* 47, 1998, p. 907.

[18] CRC Committee, *o.c.* (note 7), para. 12.

[19] M. Santos Pais, *o.c* (note 12), p. 469.

privatized the same way private services may emerge where no public services existed, in fields such as leisure, play and cultural activities. Hammarberg believes that 'what is important, however, is that the rights of the child are respected and in that regard that government will always be responsible. That responsibility cannot be privatized, which in turn raises a question about steps taken by a government to ascertain that private services for children live up to the standards of the Convention.'[20] During its discussion day on 'the private sector as service provider' (2002), the Committee stated that it:

> '[...] recognizes that State parties to the Convention on the Rights of the Child have the primary responsibility for compliance with its provisions with regard to all persons within its jurisdiction. They have a legal obligation to respect and ensure the rights of children as stipulated in the Convention, which includes the obligation to ensure that non-state service providers operate in accordance with its provisions, thus creating indirect obligations on such actors. The State continues to be bound by its obligations under the treaty, even when the provision of services is delegated to non-state actors.'[21]

35. Over 60 States Parties have made reservations upon ratification on one or more provisions of the CRC. None has made an explicit reservation on Article 31.[22] Nevertheless, some States Parties have made general reservations on all substantive articles of the Convention without specifying which provisions are affected by these limitations. Consequently these global reservations can potentially limit the implementation of Article 31 in these concerned States Parties. The Committee has consistently expressed serious concern regarding these global reservations concerning their compatibility 'with the object and purpose of the [present] Convention' (Article 51(2) of the CRC). It systematically requested States Parties that have made such global reservations on CRC to review the general nature of the reservation with a view to withdrawing it, or narrowing it.[23]

---

[20] T. Hammarberg, o.c. (note 15), p. 365.

[21] CRC Committee, Report of the thirty-first session (UN Doc. CRC/C/121, 2002), para. 653.

[22] For the updated list and full text of reservations made by States Parties upon ratification of the CRC, go to: http://www.ohchr.org/english/countries/ratification/11.htm#reservations.

[23] See for example CRC Committee, Concluding Observations: Islamic Republic of Iran (UN Doc. CRC/C/15/Add.254, 2005), paras. 6–7. The reservation of the Islamic Republic of Iran states: 'The Government of the Islamic Republic of Iran reserves the right not to apply any provisions or articles of the Convention that are incompatible with Islamic Laws and the international legislation in effect'.

3. *Scope and Meaning of Article 31*

3.1   *General Observations*

36. Though Article 31 can be easily segmented in four different human rights (*Cf. supra* Chapter II), some observations apply to the provision in general.

37. As seen earlier, the drafting of Article 31 has been largely inspired by the 1966 CESCR which by nature covers the group of rights spelled out in its title. The scope of the CRC is nevertheless broader as in addition to economic, social and cultural rights it also covers civil and political ones. The CRC Committee qualifies this particularity as 'the Convention's holistic perspective on children's rights: that they are indivisible and interrelated, and that equal importance should be attached to each and every right.'[24] Thus, Article 31 of the CRC, as any other provision of the CRC, should never be interpreted in isolation of other rights; it should be prompted by inter-linking all relevant rights recognized in the treaty.

38. The Committee has clustered Article 31 of the CRC under the title 'Education', not with the intention of limiting this provision to the right to education, but to indicate obvious strong links in this area. In its reporting guidelines, in addition to the right to education, the CRC Committee links Article 31 with the general principles of the Convention, namely the right to non-discrimination (Article 2), the principle of the best interests of the child (Article 3), the right to life, survival and development (Article 6) and the right of the child to express its views freely in all matters affecting him or her (Article 12). Obviously, in the context of implementing and monitoring Article 31, many other provisions are fundamental, such as the right to receive appropriate direction and guidance by adults in the exercise by the child of its rights (Article 5), the rights to freedom of expression, thought, conscience, religion, association and peacefully assembly (Articles 13 to 15), the right to privacy and the right to access to information (Articles 16–17).

---

[24] CRC Committee, *General Guidelines Regarding the Form and Contents of Periodic Reports to be Submitted by States Parties under Article 44, Paragraph 1(b), of the Convention* (UN Doc. CRC/C/58, 1996), para. 9.

39. In the framework of the CRC, the rights of the child to rest and leisure, to engage in play and recreational activities and to participate freely in cultural life and the arts cannot restrictively be referred to as rights belonging solely to the group of economic, social and cultural rights. In fact, Article 31, as other provisions of the CRC, also includes civil and political rights dimensions that will be looked at more in detail in the following sub-chapters. Evidently, Article 31 does not only cover protection rights but also participatory rights, many of which are based on the civil and political rights of children, as recognized in Articles 13 to 17 of the CRC.

40. As for many other provisions of the CRC, the implementation of Article 31 needs to duly take into account and respect the concept of the 'evolving capacities of the child' (Article 5) in order that he or she can properly exercise its rights.[25] Adults, including parents, early childhood and leisure professionals and teachers, need to provide the tools and an appropriate environment in order to ensure that children can, if they desire so, progressively engage freely in their leisure, recreational and cultural activities and also enjoy rest. The CRC Committee recommended in 2004:[26]

> 'The Convention on the Rights of the Child principally enshrines children's participation in all matters affecting children. Therefore, States parties must take all appropriate measures to ensure that the concept of the child as rights-holder is anchored in the child's daily life from the earliest stage: at home (and including, when applicable, the extended family); in school; in day-care facilities and in his or her community. States parties should take all appropriate measures to promote the active involvement of parents (and extended families), schools and communities at large in the promotion and creation of opportunities for young children to actively and progressively exercise their rights in their everyday activities. In this regard, special attention must be given to the freedoms of expression, thought, conscience and religion and the right to privacy of the youngest children, in accordance with their evolving capacity.'

---

[25] See R. Hodgkin and B. Holmberg, 'The evolving capacities of the child', in: A. Petren and J. Himes (eds.), *Children's rights, turning principles into practice* (Stockholm, Save the Children-Sweden and UNICEF, 2000) and G. Lansdown, *Innocenti Insight: The evolving capacities of the child* (Florence, Save the Children and UNICEF Innocenti Research Centre, 2005), 62p.
[26] CRC Committee, *Report of the Thirty-seventh Session* (UN Doc. CRC/C/143, 2005), para. 555.

41. Article 31 of the CRC is sometimes referred to as the 'forgotten right'[27] the same way some authors consider the right to take part in cultural life under Article 15 of the CESCR as a right to which 'scant attention has been paid.'[28] Cultural rights in general are frequently estimated as the least developed in terms of enforceability.[29] The four main rights of the child recognized in Article 31 have certainly been very rarely, if not never, addressed by domestic jurisdictions and consequently no consistent national jurisprudence has grown around these human rights. Regionally too there exists no jurisprudence; the international jurisprudence of the CRC Committee is still very scarce and superficial.

42. Article 31 may well be the most neglected provision by the CRC Committee since it started its monitoring work in 1991. An analysis of the 98 country-based concluding observations adopted by the Committee between 2000 and 2004 shows that only in 15 countries the CRC Committee addressed the contents of Article 31 (less than 15%), often even in a very brief and scattered manner. The reasons for this negligence may be multiple. First, States Parties often report very scarcely under Article 31, or sometimes even not at all. The same often applies to child rights advocacy groups that also neglect this area and no non-governmental organisation specifically reports on Article 31 to the CRC Committee. Further, the CRC Committee works usually under such time pressure that for purely pragmatic reasons it is pushed to neglect some aspects of the CRC. But these are not the only reasons leading to this situation. The rights recognized under Article 31 – rest, play, leisure and culture – are often perceived as a luxury in comparison to other rights whose violations bear more cruel, visible and spectacular consequences. This perception is relatively persistent, despite the wide recognition in and outside child development circles of the crucial role that rest, play, leisure and culture have for the social, cognitive and personal development of the child.[30]

---

[27] R. Hodgkin and P. Newell, *Implementation Handbook for the Convention on the Rights of the Child* (New York, UNICEF, 2002), p. 465.

[28] S. Yee, *l.c.* (note 17), p. 904.

[29] H. Niec, 'Casting the foundation for the implementation of cultural rights', in: H. Niec (ed.), *Cultural Rights and Wrongs. A Collection of Essays in Commemoration of the 50th Anniversary of the Universal Declaration of Human Rights* (Paris, UNESCO, 1999), p. 178 and A. Eide, 'Cultural Rights as Individual Human Rights', in: A. Eide *et al.* (eds), *Economic, Social and Cultural Rights*, 2nd ed. (Dordrecht/Boston/London, Kluwer Law International, 2001), p. 289.

[30] See UNICEF, *Sport, Recreation and Play* (UNICEF, New York, 2004), pp. 1–2.

43. In 2004, concerned by the lack of attention and resources provided for the implementation of Article 31 of the CRC, the CRC Committee declared[31] that it:

> '[. . .] has noted over the years that in general, insufficient attention is given and measures taken to implement the provisions of article 31 of the Convention, which guarantees 'the right of the child to rest and leisure, to engage in play and recreational activities appropriate to the age of the child and to participate freely in cultural life and the arts.' This is a concern as these rights have proved to be crucial at an early age for the sound development of each child. The right to rest is essential for children and failure to respect it can generate serious negative physical, psychological, cognitive and social consequences. The rights to leisure, play, and to a cultural and artistic life are also key human rights enabling every single young child to fully develop its potential skills, abilities and personality.'

44. Further, in order to provide increased visibility to Article 31, the CRC Committee recommended States Parties the following after its 2004 Day of General Discussion on 'Implementing child rights in early childhood':[32]

> 'In view of the insufficient attention given by States parties and others concerned to the implementation of the provisions of article 31 of the Convention, which guarantees "the right of the child to rest and leisure, to engage in play and recreational activities appropriate to the age of the child and to participate freely in cultural life and the arts", the Committee reiterates that these are key rights that enable every young child to fully develop his/her personality, talents and mental and physical abilities to their fullest potential. Recognizing that these rights are often endangered by all manner of external constraints hindering children's collective play and recreation in a stimulating and secure environment that is child-appropriate, the Committee appeals to all States parties, non-governmental organizations and private actors to identify and remove potential obstacles to the enjoyment of these rights by the youngest children, including through poverty reduction strategies. In this connection, States parties are encouraged to pay greater attention and allocate adequate resources (human and financial) to the implementation of the right to rest, leisure and play.'

45. Also since 2005, and probably as a direct result of its Day of General Discussion, the Committee has slightly enhanced its attention to Article 31 in its dialogue with States Parties.

---

[31] CRC Committee, *Report of the thirty-fifth session* (UN Doc. CRC/C/137, 2004), Annex II, para. 10.
[32] CRC Committee, *o.c.* (note 26), para. 554.

3.2   *The Right to Rest*

46. The right of the child to rest can be considered as the right that States Parties and those who have the care of children neglect the most. The right to rest is as important as other fundamental rights, such as the rights to nutrition, clothing and housing; not respecting this right can be considered a form of abuse.[33] Children who habitually suffer from insufficient or poor-quality sleep can be more vulnerable to physical and psychological health problems and to developmental, social and learning deficiencies. Research tends to show that, contrary to popular belief, adolescents (aged 10 to 17) need as much sleep, if not more, as children under the age of 10[34] and the complex and demanding developmental needs and rights of adolescents are increasingly recognized, from both an internal (biological) and an external (social, educational, environmental) point of view.[35]

47. Originally, the right to rest was recognized in the CESCR under Article 7 solely in the context of 'just and favorable conditions of work.' In the context of this provision, the Committee on Economic, Social and Cultural Rights has concentrated its work almost exclusively on the reduction of working hours and the provision of paid holidays, not the right to rest.[36] In his commentary on the Universal Declaration of Human Rights, Melander specifies that, in the context of Article 24 of the UDHR 'rest' encompasses a 'reasonable limitation of working hours.'[37] During the early stages of the drafting process of Article 31 of the CRC, Canada proposed that the right to rest and leisure be formulated as a separate right (and not along with the rights to play and participation in cultural life and the arts) as it was to be enjoyed not only in the context of work, but also in the family, in school and in the community. The text of the

---

[33] P. David, *Human rights in Youth Sports. A Critical Review of Children's Rights in Competitive Sports* (London, Routledge, 2005), p. 61.

[34] National Research Council and Institute of Medicine, *Sleep needs, patterns, and difficulties of adolescents*, Summary of a workshop, Board on Children, Youth and Families (Washington, National Research Council and Institute of Medicine, 2000).

[35] See also CRC Committee, *General Comment. No. 4: Adolescent Health and Development in the Context of the Convention on the Rights of the Child* (UN Doc. CRC/GC/2003/4, 2003).

[36] M.C.R. Craven, *The International Covenant on Economic, Social and Cultural Rights. A Perspective on its Development* (Oxford, Clarendon Press, 2002), p. 244.

[37] G. Melander, 'Article 24', in: A. Eide *et al.* (eds.), *The Universal Declaration of Human Rights: A Commentary* (Oslo, Scandinavian University Press, 1992), p. 381.

proposal requested States Parties to 'take steps to implement this right, including making reasonable limitations on school and working hours.'[38] The proposal was dropped as the number of hours weekly and yearly spent in schools varies enormously worldwide, also in relation to home work, and therefore no consensual wording could be agreed upon.

48. As seen earlier, the CRC Committee understands that in the context of the CRC, the right to rest applies to working children but similarly to other situations, including education and leisure activities.[39] Implicitly, Article 32 of the CRC on protection of children from economic exploitation recognizes the right to rest to children working legally when it requires States Parties to 'provide for appropriate regulation of the hours and conditions of employment [. . .] having regard to relevant provisions of international instruments.' In this context, these international instruments essentially refer to ILO Conventions No. 79, 90, 138 and 182. Activities undertaken under Article 31 should be, as spelled out in the text of the provision itself (para. 1), 'appropriate to the age of the child' and should not be 'excessive, entail any inadequate risk or in any way be harmful to the development, health or education of the child or involve any form of exploitation, including in areas which may seem to be primarily designed to promote the child's well-being, as in the case of sports activities or competitions', as emphasized by the then Rapporteur of the CRC Committee.[40]

49. In a few rare instances only, the CRC Committee expressed related concern when it monitored children's right to rest. In the case of Japan, for example, the Committee noted that 'children are exposed to developmental disorders due to the stress of a highly competitive educational system and the consequent lack of time for leisure, physical activities and rest [. . .] about the significant number of cases of school phobia.'[41] When reviewed for the second time, six years later, the Committee again noted that 'the excessively competitive nature of the education system has a negative effect on the children's physical and mental health and

---

[38] *Travaux Préparatoires* (UN Doc. E/CN.4/1983/62, 1983), Annex II, at Article 18: New proposal (Canada).
[39] CRC Committee, *o.c.* (note 24), para. 118.
[40] M. Santos Pais, *o.c.* (note 12) p. 468.
[41] CRC Committee, *Concluding Observations: Japan* (UN Doc. CRC/C/15/Add.90, 1998), para. 22.

hampers the development of the child to his or her fullest potential'[42] and that the measure taken by the Government after 1998 in reducing school weeks from six to five days did not lead to a decrease of stress.[43]

50. Typically, the right of the child to rest (as other rights recognized in Article 31) has been given very little, if any, attention in domestic jurisprudence. In a rare case, judged by a Dutch civil court regarding deprivation of liberty of asylum seekers in the Netherlands, the court reflected on the right to rest of child asylum-seekers.[44] Five non-governmental organisations filed a complaint on the living conditions of asylum-seekers in a refugee camp in the Netherlands, including with regard to what they considered an over-busy programme of activities for children. Child asylum-seekers were required in this camp to follow a daily mandatory programme from 8:30 to 20:30, and from 10:30 to 12:30 on week-ends. On the basis of Article 31 of the CRC, the court recalled that children have the right to rest and leisure time and ruled that these programmes were not necessarily in contravention of Article 31 of the CRC but that they could in any case be of a mandatory nature as children need to be free to choose their time of rest and leisure activities.

51. The Dutch civil court case referred above represents an interesting case of direct application of the CRC in court, as the court's decision is directly referring to part of the text of article 31 of the treaty. Nevertheless, it should not be assumed, based only on this case, that article 31 is of self-executing nature in all States parties and that the CRC is automatically part of domestic law. As a general rule, international human rights instruments are part of domestic law of countries with a civil law system, in Islamic and in Central and Eastern European countries and in most successor States of the former Soviet Union. This is not the case in most common law systems, in Scandinavia and in communist countries following the previous Soviet-style legal system.[45] Similarly, the conclusion should not be drawn that article 31 can not be used by courts

---

[42] CRC Committee, *Concluding Observations: Japan* (UN Doc. CRC/C/15/Add.231, 2004), para. 49(a).

[43] CRC Committee, *Summary Records: Japan* (UN Doc. CRC/C/SR.943, 2004), para. 7.

[44] Rechtbank 's-Gravenhage, *sector civiel recht – voorzieningenrechter*, KG 03/284, 23 April 2004.

[45] M. Nowak, *UN Covenant on Civil and Political Rights – CCPR Commentary*, 2nd revised edition, N.P. Engel, p. 59.

and implemented in countries that have no self-applicability tradition; but such action requires article 31 to be transposed explicitly in domestic legislation. In its work the CRC Committee is usually advocating for the self-executing nature of CRC and over the last 15 years it should be noted that some countries that did not in the past apply this approach (such as France, for example) have now moved towards accepting the direct application of many provisions of the CRC and other international human rights instruments.

52. Competitive sports, especially intensive training programmes, are an example of activities that by nature require important physical and psychological efforts. Respect for the right to rest is crucial for young athletes who train on a daily basis, sometimes spending more time in sports halls than in school. Young competitors sometimes have to get up early to train before school and then train again in the evening; between sports and school they potentially may have little or no time for themselves and often not enough time to rest. In 1997, Dr Michel Leglise, at that time chairman of the International Gymnastics Federation's medical committee, reiterated:

> '[A]nother vital point is the need for rest periods and plenty of sleep [ ] Children need far more sleep than adults; this must be taken into account not only in daily life, by avoiding late training sessions, but also by avoiding early morning qualifying sessions and evening competitions.'[46]

3.3   The Right to Leisure

53. The right to leisure is usually associated to the right to rest by most authors as originally they both relate to working conditions,[47] including in Article 7 of the CESCR and Article 24 of the UDHR. The CRC provides a broader frame to these provisions, but nevertheless the rights to rest and to leisure remain strongly interweaved; the assumption is that the right to leisure can only be enjoyed when the right to rest is guaranteed. Detrick specifies that the right to leisure intends to 'make it possible for the individual to cultivate his or her mind and interests.'[48] Hodgkin and

---

[46] M. Leglise, *The protection of young people involved in high-level sport. Limits on young gymnastics' involvement in high level sport* (Strasbourg, Committee for the Development of Sports, Council of Europe, 1997), p. 10.

[47] S. Detrick, *o.c.* (note 5), p. 549.

[48] *Ibid.*

Newell add that 'the right to leisure encompasses more than just having sufficient time to sleep at night [...] children need some space for
themselves between work and education.'[49] In this context, Article 16 of
the CRC is also crucial in that it guarantees the right to privacy of the
child. Leisure time intends to offer a free space for children outside of
formal settings to engage in activities of their own choice.

54. Though not systematically, the CRC Committee recommends some
States Parties to take measures to promote the right to leisure, including with regard to children with disabilities,[50] child labourers, street children[51] or child detainees.[52] The United Nations Standard Rules on the
Equalization of Opportunities for Persons with Disabilities[53] promote the
right to play of persons with disabilities (rule 4; para. 6); the United
Nations Rules for the Protection of Juveniles Deprived of their Liberty[54]
promote in paragraphs 18, 32 and 47 the right to leisure of persons below
eighteen deprived of their liberty.

3.4   The Right to Engage in Play and Recreational Activities

55. The CRC is the first and only legally binding international human
rights instrument which expressly recognizes the right to engage in play
and recreational activities. The CRC being drafted during the eighties, it
probably largely benefited from the significant body of research that
developed during the previous decades within academic, professional
and other circles providing evidence on the central role that play has
on the development of children.[55] Consensus usually exists in the recognition that play can impact positively on children's physical and psychological development. It also provides them the opportunity to develop

---

[49] R. Hodgkin and P. Newell, *o.c.* (note 27), p. 467.
[50] For example, CRC Committee, *Concluding Observations: South Africa* (UN Doc.
CRC/C/15/Add.122, 2000), paras. 34–35.
[51] For example, CRC Committee, *Concluding Observations: The Philippines* (UN Doc.
CRC/C/15/Add.258, 2005), paras. 71–72.
[52] For example, CRC Committee, *Concluding Observations: Georgia* (UN Doc. CRC/C/
15/Add.124, 2000), paras. 68–69.
[53] General Assembly resolution 48/96 of 20 December 1993.
[54] General Assembly resolution 45/113 of 14 December 1990.
[55] See for example, J. Piaget, *Play, dreams, and imitation in childhood* (New York, W.W.
Norton, 1962) and B. Sutton-Smith, *The ambiguity of play* (Cambridge, Harvard University
Press, 1997).

their social skills, including negotiations and conflict resolution, to learn self-control and autonomy, to facilitate social integration of all groups of children, and develop their creativity.

56. The right to play is different from the right to recreational activities, as 'play' refers to unstructured informal activities of children that are not controlled by adults, though they may be supervised and facilitated by them, and which do not necessarily conform to any rules. 'Recreational activities' imply a more organized and formal form of activities that in some instances can be framed by precise rules. They can be related to the school curriculum, such as sports, performing and creative arts, culture, etcetera. A similarity of both rights is that they cover activities which are based on free choice and in no way compulsory; they generally take place outside of the formal school and work settings.

57. The right to engage in play and recreational activities is linked to the civil rights of the CRC (Articles 13 to 17) and the right of the child to express its views freely in any matter affecting him or her (Article 12). Indeed, in order to ensure that children can play and engage in recreational activities, it is important that they grow up in an environment that offers space for them to develop autonomously their own play skills, under – when necessary – adult guidance and supervision. In accordance with their evolving capacities, children need to be given the possibility to enjoy their rights to freedom of expression, thought and association in order to enjoy their right to play and to engage in recreational activities. Their right to privacy and to access to information aimed at the promotion of their 'social, spiritual and moral well-being and physical and mental health', as spelled out in Article 17 of the CRC, are also crucial in this process. In the context of the right to engage in recreational activities, when appropriate, parental guidance should be provided, in light of Article 5 of the CRC, 'in a manner consistent with the evolving capacities of the child.' Such guidance should be framed notably by the aims of education (which according to the CRC Committee also embrace 'life experiences')[56] as spelled out in Article 29(1) of the CRC, especially:

> '(a) The development of the child's personality, talents and mental and physical abilities to their fullest potential; [. . .]

---

[56] CRC Committee, *General Comment No. 1: The aims of education* (UN Doc. CRC/GC/2001/1, 2001), para. 2.

(d) The preparation of the child for responsible life in a free society, in the spirit of understanding, peace, tolerance, equality of sexes, and friendship among all peoples, ethnic, national and religious groups and persons of indigenous origin; [. . .].'

58. As seen above,[57] States Parties need to ensure that protection and participation rights of children are equally respected in the context of play and recreational activities. This is especially relevant in the context of, firstly, play that should remain based on spontaneity, freedom and informality and also of, secondly, recreational activities that need to be chosen by children and parents on the basis of freedom of choice. At the same time, both play and recreational activities need to be undertaken under 'competent supervision' (Article 3(3) of the CRC), and in the case of the latter, in conformity 'with the standards established by competent authorities, particularly, in the areas of safety, health [. . .]' (Article 3(3) of the CRC). Further, the CRC clearly calls for children engaging in play and recreational activities 'appropriate to the age of the child' (Article 31(1)). This is a fundamental requirement of the CRC as it means that adults should not impose on – or even propose – children play or recreational activities that are not fully adapted to their age, maturity, capacities and level of development. It is also a reaffirmation that children are not miniature adults and should be respected as they are and with their own limitations. This is particularly relevant in the field of sports and performing arts where children, especially gifted ones, can potentially be pushed into adult environment without necessarily being properly prepared to deal with the related challenges and demands.

59. In its jurisprudence, as well as in its General Discussion Day on 'Implementing Child Rights in Early Childhood' (2004), the Committee recognized the importance of play and recreational activities for the sound development of children. It has expressed concern in some instances at the 'inadequacy of budget allocations'[58] in these areas or at the 'lack of affordable sports facilities and other recreational programmes'.[59]

---

[57] *Cf. supra* Chapter III, Section 3.1.

[58] For example, CRC Committee, *Concluding Observations: Armenia* (UN Doc. CRC/C/15/Add.225, 2004), para. 48 or CRC Committee, *Concluding Observations: Portugal* (UN Doc. CRC/C/15/Add.162, 2001), para. 44.

[59] For example, CRC Committee, *Concluding Observations: Kingdom of the Netherlands (Netherlands Antilles)* (UN Doc. CRC/C/15/Add.186, 2002), para. 54.

In other States Parties, the Committee identified the lack of recreational and play areas as a serious concern.[60]

60. Often there is a general assumption in societies that recreational activities can only be positive for the development of children. This is usually the case of sports which typically are perceived in many circles as only beneficial to the child. This is probably generally the case, but at the same time one should recognize that the rights of children involved in sports, especially in competitive sports, can be threatened by the excessive expectations put on them by concerned adults (this is not unique to sport as it might also happen in other situations, such as educational achievement or performing arts).[61]

61. Sports and public authorities have the responsibility under the CRC to ensure full respect of child rights, including within the frame of sports activities. Under the treaty they also commit to take necessary measures to this aim (this would also apply for example to the involvement of children in the fashion business or performing arts). Potential threats to young athletes include excessive intensive training resulting in chronic injuries, psychological, sexual and physical abuse, doping and neglect of education. Scarcity of research and data in this area still limits awareness on these issues, but existing research points out generally that between 1 and 10 percent of young athletes experience various forms of sexual abuse or violence and 2 to 10 percent of young athletes use illicit doping products. Trafficking and sale of young talents also exist between Africa and Latin America and Western Europe in football; between Central America and the USA and Canada in baseball. Young prospects from developing countries are sometimes sent illegally by unscrupulous intermediaries to industrialized countries on try-outs in wealthy sports clubs; most of them will not be selected and will be left to their own, sometimes being forced into clandestinity and even engage in criminal activities in order to survive.

62. Sports authorities also need to respect the right of the child to freedom of association (Article 14 of the CRC). When talented young athletes

---

[60] For example, CRC Committee, *Concluding Observations: Mozambique* (UN Doc. CRC/C/15/Add.172, 2002), para. 58 or CRC Committee, *Concluding Observations: Marshall Islands* (UN Doc. CRC/C/15/Add.139, 2000), para. 52.

[61] For further analysis on this issue: P. David, *o.c.* (note 33), pp. 213–232.

want to change clubs, their original club may request that a compensa-
tion fee be paid to recompense its work in developing the athletes' potential before it releases them. Sporting authorities have allowed and even
legitimized these transfer practices, which are especially common in the
most popular sports (football, basketball, etcetera). But they may severely
infringe the right to freedom of association of young athletes by condi-
tioning their freedom of movement with the payment of a transfer sum.
Young athletes can be transferred against their will if their club wants
to make profit through selling its players; they may also be frustrated
in their desire to change clubs if the transfer sum requested is considered excessive by other clubs. Such serious threats to the freedom of
association of young athletes have been denounced and brought to court
in both Belgium[62] and Luxembourg, and subsequently sports associations
in these countries have had to change their transfer regulations.[63]

63. Since the seventies, a certain number of international non-governmental organisations have developed soft law instruments regarding
issues covered by Article 31 of the CRC (especially in the field of play
and recreational activities). The most significant ones are probably the
'IPA Declaration of a Child's Right to Play' adopted in 1977 (last revised
in 1989) by the International Association for the Child's Right to Play
(IPA)[64] and the 'Charter for Leisure' adopted in 2000 by the World Leisure
and Recreation Association.[65] The IPA Declaration provides from the
organisational point of view some insight on the definition of 'play'.
Noting that play has always existed, IPA considers play as important as
nutrition, health and education for the development of children. It emphasizes the nature of play as being 'instinctive, voluntary and spontaneous.'
The World Leisure and Recreation Association highlights the importance
of leisure for the 'quality of life' and considers it 'as important as health
and education.'

---

[62] See for example: Civ. Verviers (4e ch.), 4 January 1994, *Journal du Droit des Jeunes*, no. 138, p. 29.
[63] R. Blanpain, *Les gladiateurs du sport, la mafia du sport* (Brussels, La Charte, 1993), 200p.
[64] Full text available on: http://www.ipascotland.org.uk.
[65] Full text available on: http://www.worldleisure.org.

3.5   *The Right to Participate Freely in Cultural Life and the Arts*

64. The wording of the right to participate freely in cultural life and the arts is inspired by the UDHR (Article 24) and the CESCR (Article 15(1)). Though the UDHR refers to the right to 'freely' participate in the cultural life, the CESCR, which was adopted almost two decades later, does not include such reference to freedom of choice and of the freedom of creative artists (though four other articles of the CESCR refer explicitly to the word 'freely'). Three decades later, the CRC has re-introduced this concept, which is crucial, both in terms of the right to freedom of choice and the freedom of creative artists in general, but additionally in the process of acquisition of autonomy of the child. Whereas the UDHR and CRC explicitly refer to the 'arts' as an addition to 'culture', the CESCR drops the word 'arts', implicitly considering that it is part of 'culture'. Further, the UDHR refers to the right to participate in the cultural life 'of the community', a word – that could be interpreted as restricting this right – that both the CESCR and the CRC have dropped, leaving the application of this right entirely open.

65. Among the five traditional groups of rights (civil, political, economic, social and cultural), several authors believe that cultural rights are the ones that have been given the least attention by governments, the judiciary and academic circles.[66] This relative neglect added to the broad nature of the concept of 'cultural rights' has led to a difficulty to narrowly provide for a strict legal definition of 'the right to participate freely in cultural life'.[67] The Committee on Economic, Social and Cultural Rights, at the occasion of its General Discussion on 'The Right to Take Part in Cultural Life as Recognized in Article 15 of the Covenant' (1992) also expressed the view that cultural rights 'were in a sense "underdeveloped", largely because of a lack of clarity about their legal nature and content'.[68]

---

[66] S. Yee, *l.c.* (note 17), p. 904; H. Niec., *o.c.* (note 29), p. 178; G. Melander, *o.c.* (note 37), p. 429.

[67] H. Niec, *o.c.* (note 29), p. 178.

[68] CESCR Committee, *Summary record* (UN Doc. E/C.12/1992/SR.17, 1992), para. 5.

66. Yee considers that the 'right to take part in cultural life' as defined in the CESCR encompasses three overlapping and equally valid concepts:[69]

(1) 'culture' in the classic highbrow sense, meaning the traditional canon of art, literature, music, theatre, architecture, and so on;

(2) 'culture' in a more pluralist sense, meaning all those products and manifestations of creative and expressive drives, a definition which encompasses not only 'high' culture but also more mass phenomenons such as commercial television and radio, the popular press, contemporary and folk music, handicrafts and organized sports; and,

(3) 'culture' in the anthropological sense, meaning, not simply the products of artifacts of creativity and expression (as envisaged by the first two definitions) but, rather, a society's underlying and characteristic pattern of thought – its 'way of life' – from which these and all social manifestations spring.

67. Stavenhagen endorses this approach and summarizes it as: a) culture as a capital, b) culture as creativity and c) culture as a total way of life.[70] Dinstein considers that 'culture is a flexible term, which can be employed either in a broad sense covering the whole gamut of human knowledge or in a narrower meaning depending on the specific content.'[71] Many authors also distinguish the right to cultural life as both an individual and collective right.[72] It is considered an individual right when referred to as the right of every human being to participate, access and enjoy culture. It becomes a collective one, when a specific culture can only be enjoyed in or by a given community with others and that community must have the possibility to preserve, protect and develop what it shares in common.[73]

---

[69] S. Yee, l.c. (note 17), p. 905.

[70] R. Stavenhagen, 'Cultural rights: a social science perspective', in: H. Niec (ed.), l.c. (note 29), p. 1.

[71] Y. Dinstein, 'Cultural rights', Israel Yearbook on Human Rights 9, 1979, p. 74.

[72] For example, S. Yee, l.c. (note 17), p. 917.

[73] R. Stevenhagen, 'Cultural rights and universal human rights', in: A. Eide et al. (eds.), l.c. (note 29), p. 68.

68. A number of authors bridge the individual right to participate in cultural life with the collective one to cultural identity.[74] Referring to minority and indigenous groups, Stavenhagen[75] considers that

> 'Culture is also seen as a coherent self-contained system of values and symbols that a specific cultural group reproduces over time and which provides individuals with the required signposts and meanings for behaviour and social relationships in every day life.'

69. In the context of the CRC, collective rights of minority and indigenous groups are recognized in its Article 30, which states:

> '[I]n those States in which ethnic, religious or linguistic minorities or persons of indigenous origin exist, a child belonging to such a minority or who is indigenous shall not be denied the right, in community with other members of his or her group, to enjoy his or her own culture, to profess and practise his or her own religion, or to use his or her own language.'

70. Though the passive style of the wording of this provision remains relatively weak ('shall not be denied the right'), this provision is nevertheless the first – and still the only one – of legally binding nature under international law that grants human rights to indigenous people and groups. Indigenous children are granted the right to enjoy their own culture, religion and language; implicitly States have the obligation to refrain from interfering in this regard.

71. The 1976 UNESCO Recommendation on Participation by the People at Large in Cultural Life and their Contribution to It defines 'participation in cultural life' as:

> 'the concrete opportunities guaranteed for all – groups or individuals – to express themselves freely, to act, and engage in creative activities with a view to the full development of their personalities, a harmonious life and the cultural progress of society.'[76]

---

[74] For example, J.H. Burgers, 'The Right to Cultural Identity', pp. 251–253; and R. Stavenhagen, 'The Right to Cultural Identity', pp. 255–258, in: J. Bertin *et al.* (eds.), *Human Rights in a Pluralist World: Individuals and Collectivities* (Westport, Meckler, 1990) or S. Yee, *l.c.* (note 17), pp. 918–919.

[75] R. Stevenhagen, *o.c.* (note 73), p. 66.

[76] Recommendation on Participation by the People at Large in Cultural Life and their Contribution to It, adopted at UNESCO General Conference, Nairobi, 26 November 1976.

72. This definition links the enjoyment of the right to participation in cultural life to the full development of the personality; a link that also exists indirectly in the CRC through the provision of Article 29(1)(a) that provides for '[t]he development of the child's personality, talents and mental and physical abilities to their fullest potential.'

73. The right of the child to participate freely in cultural life and the arts also relates to the right of the child to access appropriate information as recognized in Article 17 of the CRC that obliges States to:

'(a) Encourage the mass media to disseminate information and material of social and cultural benefit to the child and in accordance with the spirit of article 29;

(b) Encourage international co-operation in the production, exchange and dissemination of such information and material from a diversity of cultural, national and international sources;

(c) Encourage the production and dissemination of children's books;

(d) Encourage the mass media to have particular regard to the linguistic needs of the child who belongs to a minority group or who is indigenous;

(e) Encourage the development of appropriate guidelines for the protection of the child from information and material injurious to his or her well-being, bearing in mind the provisions of articles 13 and 18.'

74. As recognized in Article 17, States Parties need to find in the context of implementing Article 31 of the CRC a sound balance between the right of the child to freedom of information and his or her right to be protected 'from information and material injurious to his or her well-being, bearing in mind the provisions of Articles 13 and 18 [of the CRC].' The CRC Committee essentially refers in its jurisprudence to three types of injurious information and materials: those related to racism, xenophobia and other forms of intolerance, to sexual abuse and exploitation, and to violence.[77] Article 17 applies to all forms of information, including oral, visual and the Internet. Any form of censorship needs to be well founded and based on existing States' legislation and related obligations, on responsibilities, rights and duties of parents as well as the evolving capacities of the child and its right to exercise his or her own rights (Article 5 of the CRC).

---

[77] R. Hodgkin and P. Newell, o.c. (note 27), pp. 236–238.

75. So far, the CRC Committee has not given much flesh on the bones of the right of the child to participate freely in cultural life and the arts. In a few concluding observations on State Parties' compliance with the CRC, it has referred to 'the children's access to quality leisure facilities like sport centres and public libraries'[78] or it has recommended a State Party to 'organize cultural after school activities such as drawing, plastic arts, dance and music, in participation with children, and to make available free and accessible public sport facilities'.[79]

76. During its Day of General Discussion on 'The Rights of Indigenous Children', the Committee discussed the collective rights of indigenous children to enjoy, develop and preserve their own culture, including their own language, history, values.[80] The Committee also emphasized during its Day of General Discussion on the 'Child and the Media' the importance of providing access to children to libraries, in the spirit of Article 17(c) of the CRC that requires States Parties to 'encourage the production and dissemination of children's books'.[81]

77. In the view of Hodgkin and Newell, the meaning of the right to freely participate in cultural life and the arts is twofold and needs to be child-oriented and specific: 1) the right of children to join adults in their cultural and artistic pursuits and 2) the right to child-centred culture and arts. They state:

> '[C]hildren should not be barred from adults events, or performances without good reason (for example because the child might be psychologically harmed or because young infants might disrupt the performance). In addition, children should be given opportunities to participate in all forms of cultural and artistic activity as well as enjoy performances and exhibitions specifically for their pleasure.'[82]

78. Hodgkin and Newell raise the fundamental issue: the right to freely participate in cultural life and the arts, like many other child rights, is on the one hand identical to the right recognized to adults, but on the

---

[78] CRC Committee, *Concluding Observations: Armenia* (UN Doc. CRC/C/15/Add.225, 2004), para. 56.

[79] CRC Committee, *o.c.* (note 59), para. 55.

[80] CRC Committee, *Report of the Thirty-fourth Session* (UN Doc. CRC/C/133, 2004), paras. 608–624.

[81] CRC Committee, *Report of theTthirteenth Session* (UN Doc. CRC/C/57, 1996), paras. 242–257.

[82] R. Hodgkin and P. Newell, *o.c.* (note 27), p. 470.

other hand its child specific dimension needs to be acknowledged, especially in relation to protection and participation rights. Appropriate assessment and respect for the evolving capacities of the child and his or her right to express freely views are in these context essential processes for proper implementation and respect.